Cornerstones of Freedom

The Story of
THE UNDERGROUND RAILROAD

By R. Conrad Stein

Illustrated by Ralph Canaday

CHILDRENS PRESS ™

CHICAGO

Library of Congress Cataloging in Publication Data

Stein, R. Conrad.
   The story of the underground railroad.

   (Cornerstones of freedom:
   SUMMARY: Discusses the network of groups and
individuals throughout Ohio and the New England
states who aided slaves escaping from their captivity
during the nineteenth century.
   1.   Underground railroad—Juvenile literature.
2.   Slavery—United States—Anti-slavery movements—
Juvenile literature. |1.   Underground railroad.
2.   Slavery—Anti-slavery movements| I.   Canaday, Ralph.
II.   Title.   III.   Series.
E450.S83   326'.0973   81-3801
ISBN 0-516-04643-8   AACR2

Tice Davids ran for his life. Behind him his master tramped over the fields. The master carried a shotgun. Davids raced up a hill. Thorns tore his clothing and scratched his skin. At the top of the hill, the runaway slave stopped and gasped. He saw what seemed like a miracle. Below him, the broad Ohio River flowed gently. This river had been his goal for days—ever since he had broken away from his Kentucky plantation. It was his gateway to freedom.

Davids had no time to stop and stare at the river. He could hear his master's voice in the distance behind him. "Davids! Stop where you are!" Tice Davids ran down the hill and plunged into the icy water.

Tice's master searched the bank for a rowboat. Finding one, he began to row across the Ohio. As he rowed, he kept an eye on his slave, swimming in the current.

The Ohio River was the border between the state of Kentucky and the state of Ohio. Slavery was illegal in Ohio. But the law allowed a slave owner to enter another state in order to catch a runaway slave. Davids' master had the legal right to capture him and take him back to Kentucky in chains.

Still Davids swam the river. Other slaves had told him that he would find help in Ohio. There he would find people who believed slavery was sinful. They had helped other slaves escape. Davids splashed out of the water and struggled up the bank. Ahead he saw a dozen white frame houses. He ran toward them, hoping he would find help. Davids was lucky. He had reached the town of Ripley, Ohio. The people of Ripley hated slavery.

The Rankin family lived in Ripley. John Rankin was a huge farmer who had seven sons. The entire family hated even the idea of slavery. During the day each family member took a turn keeping an eye on the river. They watched for runaway slaves. At night the Rankins left a lantern burning on their porch. The light was a signal. It told fleeing slaves that help could be found in this house.

Davids ran through a back street. Suddenly he heard someone call, "Over here! Over here!" He

looked up and saw one of Rankin's sons. The young man was holding open the door of the Rankin house. He motioned Davids inside.

The boat rowed by the slave owner bumped into the mud on the Ohio side of the river. The slave owner climbed out. He was sure he had his slave cornered. Capturing him now would be an easy task. But after a four-hour search, the slave owner stood on the main street of Ripley scratching his head in confusion. His slave was nowhere to be found. And no one in the tiny town claimed to have seen him.

Tice Davids was hiding in the cellar of John Rankin's house. Later that night, Rankin gave Davids some money and food. He told him of another house, ten miles up the road, where he could find shelter. Davids was amazed to discover that an entire network of houses where he could find help was spread out between the town of Ripley, Ohio, and his final destination—Canada.

Davids escaped from his master in 1831. He was just one of thousands who broke the chains of slavery in the years before the Civil War. But Davids' escape is remembered because it helped create a name for the escape route. When Davids' bewildered owner returned to Kentucky, he told a neighbor

about Davids' disappearance. The slave owner said that Davids had slipped away when he was almost in his grasp. "I don't know how he did it," said the owner. "He must have gone off on some underground road."

Another slave overheard his master. Soon slaves all over the South spoke in hushed tones about the underground road up North. Somehow the words "underground road" became "underground railroad," and the new term was born. The thousands of heroic men and women who daily risked their lives to help slaves on the path to freedom suddenly had a name. They were all agents of the Underground Railroad.

The Underground Railroad became one of the great adventures in American history. It was a railroad in the sense that it transported people, but it had no tracks or cars. And it had only one destination—freedom.

Slaves had attempted to escape captivity ever since they were first brought to North America in the 1600s. Some of them managed to break away from their masters and live in small colonies in the swamps and forests. Other runaways discovered they were accepted by Indian tribes.

The first spike in the Underground Railroad was driven by the very first American who helped a slave reach freedom. Exactly when that happened is unknown, but it certainly goes back to the very beginnings of United States history. As early as 1796, President George Washington, who owned slaves, wrote a letter on the subject to a friend. In the letter Washington complained that one of his servants had escaped and was living in New Hampshire under the protection of the people of a certain town. The townspeople had not only helped the slave escape, but they were willing to fight to keep him free. The president wrote that he would not order the authorities to capture the slave because he was afraid such an act would "excite a mob or a riot."

Soon after the Revolutionary War, the United States became divided between the free states of the North and the slave states of the South. It was the start of bitter feelings between pro-slavery and anti-slavery Americans. At first the voices raised against slavery were nothing more than a whisper. Still, thousands of Americans in both the North and the South believed that slavery was evil. Many of these people devoted their lives to abolishing, or removing, it from their country. Some of these people reasoned that the best way to destroy slavery was to help slaves escape to freedom. Their courage created the Underground Railroad.

When the term Underground Railroad came into use, the anti-slavery agents began using railroad language to describe their work. Thus, those who served as guides for escaped slaves became "conductors." The houses giving shelter to runaways were called "stations." The man or woman who owned the house was the "stationmaster." And the escaped slaves were the "passengers."

A few famous Underground Railroad names will always be remembered. But most agents lived and worked in secrecy. Today we think of the men and women who were devoted to helping slaves escape as heroes. Before the Civil War, however, anyone assisting an escaped slave was committing a dangerous criminal act. If caught, he could be sent to prison. He could even be put to death.

Easily the most dangerous job on the Underground Railroad was being a conductor. The conductor's task was to journey to the South, help slaves break away from their masters, and take them to the North. In the slave states, conductors risked being put to death by hanging.

One famous conductor was a white man from the

South named James Fairfield. Fairfield had grown up on a plantation in Virginia.

His family owned many slaves. When he was a child, Fairfield's best friend was a black slave boy named Bill. James and Bill fished and swam together. It didn't matter to either of them that one was a slave and the other free. As they grew older, however, they both began to understand how wicked it was that one was free to leave the plantation while the other was not. Even though Bill belonged to Fairfield's uncle, the friends made plans for Bill's escape. One day when Fairfield left the plantation for a trip, he took Bill along and smuggled him all the way to Canada, where slavery did not exist.

In Canada, and in black communities in the Northern states, Fairfield met other escaped slaves. Many of them asked him to find and free members of their families who were still held captive down South. They were even willing to pay for his help. Almost always, Fairfield agreed to help. He became one of the most successful conductors on the Underground Railroad. He lived a life of daring. Once he was shot and wounded. On another occasion he was caught in an effort to free slaves. He was forced to serve a five-year prison sentence in Kentucky.

To get inside plantation grounds, Fairfield often posed as a slave trader. He knew the ways of the South and spoke with a genuine Virginia accent. Because of this, he would often be invited to eat and spend the night in a slave owner's home. Fairfield would agree. But in the morning, he and several of the man's slaves would have disappeared. In one famous escape, Fairfield organized twenty-eight slaves into a phantom funeral procession. The coffin the men carried was empty. Using this disguise, the slaves marched through the main street of a Southern town. Once out of town, they dropped the empty coffin and raced into the woods.

The most fearless conductors on the Underground Railroad were the many blacks who regularly journeyed to the South to assist their people. Most were runaway slaves themselves. On their every trip to a slave state they faced hanging or being recaptured and forced back into a lifetime of slavery.

The cleverest and bravest of all the conductors we know about was a black woman named Harriet Tubman. She was born a slave on a farm in Maryland. When she was thirteen, her master—in a drunken rage—hit her on the head with a brass paperweight. For three days she lay in a coma, hovering between life and death. She finally awoke. But for the rest of

her life she was troubled by a strange form of sleeping sickness. Without warning, she would fall into a deep sleep. When she awoke, she was unaware that she had passed out. Despite these spells, Harriet Tubman became the Underground Railroad's most famous conductor.

When she was nineteen, Harriet sneaked away from her owner's farm. Traveling only at night and avoiding roads, she headed north. She did this by following the North Star. Harriet had strong faith in God. Before her escape, she had spent many hours in prayer and deep thought. "I had this out in my mind," she once said. "There was one of two things I had a *right* to—liberty and death; if I could not have one I would have the other."

After a long and dangerous journey, Harriet Tubman arrived in Philadelphia. There she believed that God spoke to her. He commanded her to return to the South and help other slaves reach freedom. Just a few months after her escape, Harriet went back to her old farm. She brought her sister and her sister's two children back north with her. This was the beginning of a brilliant career. Harriet was to take more than three hundred passengers on rides through the Underground Railroad. Just the mention of her name made Southern slave owners furious. At one time there were rewards on her head totaling more than $40,000.

Harriet was a master of every trick in the conductor's trade. When necessary, she dressed men in

women's clothing and women in men's. She often
stole a slave owner's horse and wagon along with his
slaves. Then she hid the runaways under fruits and
vegetables and innocently drove the wagon down the
road. One night when her pursuers were close
behind, she hid a group of slaves under a pile of
manure. She gave them straws to breathe through.
On another trip she confused a posse chasing her by
having her group board a train that was heading
south. Certainly no runaways would ride a train
south, and the men of the posse let the group go. At
the next stop, the party of slaves got off the train
and continued the walk north.

Like Moses in the Bible, Harriet Tubman led her
people out of bondage. Long before she died at the
age of ninety-two, she had earned the name "The
Moses of her People."

When an escaped slave finally arrived in the Northern states, his flight did not end. He was still a fugitive slave. As early as 1793, Congress passed a Fugitive Slave Law that said owners were allowed to capture fugitive slaves wherever they might be in the United States. Under the law, anyone assisting a fugitive could be punished.

In the South, slaves were expensive. A strong slave cost two thousand dollars or more. When a slave escaped, his owner usually tried desperately to get him back. In most cases, the owner did not pursue the slave himself. Instead, he hired professional slave catchers to hunt down the escapee. The slave catchers were crafty, ruthless men. Many of them had criminal records. Often, however, they were outwitted by agents of the Underground Railroad.

Many Underground stations had secret rooms where a slave could hide. One house even had a tunnel leading from the cellar to the woods outside. Some agents worked as peddlers. The horse-drawn wagons they drove had false bottoms that could conceal two or three fugitive slaves.

In the Northern border states, a constant war of nerves went on between stationmasters trying to hide runaways and slave catchers trying to capture

them. One story from that period told of a station-master who was also a tavern keeper. One day a slave catcher came into his tavern asking if anyone had seen a fugitive he had been chasing. The tavern keeper claimed he had seen the slave just fifteen minutes earlier. He added that the slave was wounded and should be easy to catch. So he suggested that the slave catcher have a glass of beer before continuing his chase. The slave catcher agreed, and the tavern keeper poured him a beer— then another, and another, and another. Soon the slave catcher passed out on the floor. The slave, who had been hiding in the attic of the building, hurried on to the next station.

Religious groups often aided escaped slaves. The most active of these were the slavery-hating Quakers. Quakers did have one handicap in their dealings with ruthless slave catchers. They could not lie. To a Quaker, telling even the smallest fib was a sin.

One Quaker woman got around this by calling on still another Quaker belief. The woman was a stationmaster, and one night a sheriff and a slave catcher pounded on her door. The sheriff had a warrant. He demanded to search the house for a fugitive slave. The woman said there was no slave in the house. Actually, the slave was hiding underneath her husband's bed. The sheriff told the slave catcher it would be a waste of time to search the house because Quakers never lie. After the two men left, the woman's husband was shocked at how she had so boldly told a lie. The woman explained she had not lied at all. According to her Quaker beliefs, there was no such thing as a slave. All men and women were born free. So she was actually telling the truth when she claimed there was no slave in the house.

The safest havens for runaway slaves in the United States were in the black communities that grew up in the Northern states. These towns and neighborhoods were made up mainly of former slaves. Some of them had bought their freedom. Some had been given their freedom by an owner. And some had run away so long ago that their owners had given up trying to capture them. The communities of free blacks accepted all runaways. They were also willing to fight to keep a fugitive free. Only a very foolish slave catcher would enter a settlement of former slaves to try to capture one and send him back to a life of slavery.

The Underground Railroad had dozens of routes

through Ohio and the New England states. Usually the end of those routes was Canada. Slavery did not exist in Canada.

Slave catchers were not allowed to enter the country to try to capture a fugitive. Once a slave set foot in Canada, he was forever free. A favorite song among slaves included these words:

> Oh righteous Father,
> Wilt thou not pity me,
> And aid me to Canada
> Where all the slaves are free.

One of the great men of the Underground Railroad was a Quaker named Levi Coffin. He lived in southern Indiana. Coffin had grown up in North Carolina. He remembered riding with his father one day when he was seven years old. They passed a line of slaves being driven in chains to a market. "My father addressed the slaves pleasantly," wrote Coffin, "and then asked, 'Well, boys, why do they chain you?' One of the men whose countenance betrayed unusual intelligence and whose expression denoted the deepest sadness replied: 'They have taken us away from our wives and children and they chain us lest we should make our escape and go back to them.' "

Coffin could never forget the sight of those slaves in chains. How evil was the system, he thought, that would condemn them to a life in chains from the very moment they were born. Coffin became a lifelong enemy of slavery. At the age of fourteen he helped his first slave to escape.

Although no records were kept, it has been said that as many as three thousand fugitive slaves passed through Levi Coffin's station near the Ohio River. It is no wonder that Coffin was often called the "President" of the Underground Railroad.

Exactly how many slaves escaped to freedom through the Underground Railroad is unknown. During the slave era, the governor of Mississippi claimed that between 1810 and 1850 the South lost one hundred thousand slaves valued at more than thirty million dollars. That figure is probably high, but there is no doubt that the Underground Railroad was beginning to shake the institution of slavery.

In 1850 the Southerners in Congress pushed through a new Fugitive Slave Law. It provided harsh punishments to anyone assisting a runaway slave. But that law did not stop the agents of the Underground Railroad. In the decade before the Civil War, the Railroad was at its busiest.

In the 1850s the bitter feelings between pro-slavery and anti-slavery Americans swept the country. Thousands of people demanded that slavery be abolished immediately. These people came to be called abolitionists. One abolitionist was a runaway slave named Frederick Douglass. Douglass had such power as a speaker that he overwhelmed audiences. He won converts to the abolitionist cause wherever he spoke. The voices that once had whispered against slavery were beginning to roar.

In 1858 Abraham Lincoln made a famous speech.

In it he stated that the United States could no longer exist half slave and half free. "A house divided against itself cannot stand," said Lincoln. Three years later Lincoln was president and the United States exploded into the bloody Civil War.

While the war raged, Lincoln signed the Emancipation Proclamation, which ended slavery—at least in those areas controlled by Union forces. It also ended the work of the Underground Railroad in the North. Now there was no such thing as a fugitive slave. No people were ever more delighted to lose their jobs than the anti-slavery agents of the Underground Railroad.

The heroes of the Underground Railroad had helped to destroy the institution of slavery. These Americans—both black and white—risked their lives and their freedom to bring some light into an otherwise dark chapter of the history of the United States.

About the Author

R. Conrad Stein was born and grew up in Chicago. He enlisted in the Marine Corps at the age of eighteen, and served for three years. He then attended the University of Illinois, where he received a Bachelor's Degree in history. He later studied in Mexico and earned a Master of Fine Arts degree from the University of Guanajuato.

The study of history is Mr. Stein's hobby. Since he finds it to be an exciting subject, he tries to bring the excitement of history to his readers. He is the author of many other books, articles, and short stories written for young people.

About the Artist

Ralph Canaday has been involved in all aspects of commercial art since graduation from the Art Institute of Chicago in 1959. He is an illustrator, designer, painter, and sculptor whose work has appeared in many national publications, textbooks, and corporate promotional material. Mr. Canaday lives in Hanover Park, Illinois, with his wife Arlene, who is also in publishing.